GW00362688

This true story of the Mountain Cow, provides the reader with unique insights to farming life in nineteen eighties' County Leitrim, Ireland. After a difficult calving, the Mountain Cow is paralysed. Sarah cares for the cow day and night for many weeks. She knows that cows in this distressing condition are usually "put down" or dispatched to the factory after a few days. Sarah is growing increasingly worried and desperate about the situation. The Mountain Cow has not stood up for an extraordinary one hundred and twenty days. After repeated efforts to save her involving folk remedies, lifting and massaging have apparently failed, what fate now awaits the Mountain Cow?

The Mountain Cow

A rural tale of ups and downs on a Leitrim farm

R.M. McHugh

This story records real events which took place thirty years ago.
Sarah still lives alone on the farm. Names have been changed.

Published by:
Thornhill Publishing
51 Thornhill Park
Derry
BT 48 8PB
Northern Ireland
ISBN 978-1-5272-3888-6

Printer:
Iprint Design and Print
16 J Pennyburn Industrial Estate
Derry, BT 48 0LU

Contents

1
The Calving

There were many happenings in the life of Sarah who was now in her mid-fifties. Sarah had worked the small farm with her husband Pat for thirty years. Pat was dead for seven years now and their four children were grown up and gone. Sarah still continued to work the small farm after everyone was gone. The children knew all about the ups and downs of the daily running of the farm. Sarah kept twelve cows in all and Whiz, her eldest son was a great shepherd.

It was the day before Christmas Eve when he said, "the

Mountain Cow will calve tonight."

Sarah thought, "this is good for Whiz will be here," as the calving was the thing that frightened Sarah the most.

Whiz knew when every cow was going to calve as he had helped Sarah since he was a small boy. As night approached Whiz knew it would be late when she calved so he summoned his friend Christy who lived nearby. Soon Christy arrived and noticing that Sarah was tired he exclaimed, "go to bed Sarah, you need a rest and Whiz and myself will keep an eye on things."

Sarah was glad as she was very tired and she left them to it. She climbed the long winding stairs to her bedroom in the far end of the house. Her bedroom was large and her bed was situated where she could look out on the tall tree tops. She often watched a squirrel jumping from branch to branch in search of nuts. When the snow and ice came, she would watch the patterns that formed on the branches. She could see the sky through the branches, sometimes it was blue, at other times clouds rolled by. From her bedroom, she could hear any strange sounds in the byre.

Downstairs Christy and Whiz made themselves comfortable by the stove, thinking to themselves that they might have to sit the night through. Whiz made many trips to the byre from the comfortable kitchen to see how the Mountain Cow was progressing. They talked about football, politics and the price of cattle at the marts. They made tea and felt drowsy with the heat coming from the stove.

"I'll go and have a look at her" said Whiz, "in case we fall asleep".

This time he came back quickly and called out to Christy, "come fast, the calf is coming."

Back upstairs, Sarah hadn't slept any and could hear what was going on. She thanked God that the calf was coming and thought, "Christy and Whiz will get a few hours sleep after all."

There was complete silence in the byre and Sarah thought this was strange, because if everything was alright, Whiz would let her know by shouting the good news from the bottom of the stairs. After some time, Sarah could hear quick footsteps coming from the byre and into the house. Then she heard someone dialling the phone and she knew something had gone wrong. She heard Whiz ask if "Mr Geff was in?"

Sarah got out of bed and came fast down the long winding stairs. She tripped but kept on her feet. She saw Whiz standing in the hall and panic all over his face.

"What is wrong Whiz?" she called out.

"We have been unable to take the calf. He is dead and the cow is in danger of dying too."

Sarah went pale and her heart was beating louder. She

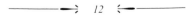

thought, "Oh God what will we do as it is well into the night?" "Did you get Mr. Geff?" she asked Whiz.

"He is on his way."

It was now one o'clock. Mr. Geff, who was the local vet, had been many times on Sarah's farm. He often had to come in the middle of the night. One night, Sarah remembered Mr Geff coming to a difficult calving and he decided he would have to operate on the cow in order to save the life of both the cow and the calf. That was a difficult night for Sarah as she had to take a table from the kitchen and set it up in the byre. She had to get a clean white sheet and spread it over the table so that Mr Geff could put his instruments on it. She watched Mr Geff freeze the side of the cow. She then watched him insert a cut nine inches long down the side of the cow and very skilfully take a lovely bull calf out on the cow's side. He stitched the cow, gave her penicillin and the whole operation was very successful.

She heard the Land Rover go past. Christy and Whiz were back in the byre. Mr Geff looked at the Mountain Cow and said "I'm afraid I'm too late, I will not be able to save the calf".

Silently Mr. Geff took the calf with the help of Christy and Whiz. All three of them stood and lamented the dead calf. Whiz felt bad as he and Sarah always rejoiced when a cow calved, this time they would not. Mr. Geff was leaving now.

"Put some comfortable straw around the cow. She should be on her feet in the morning", he said.

Christy and Whiz did as they were told and having left the byre, Sarah called out that she had tea made. Christy drank the tea quickly and left to get a few hours sleep. Whiz stayed a short while with Sarah and then left too.

Whiz was married to a local girl who was staying at her parents' house with their small son. Sarah was on her

own now. She climbed the long winding stairs again to her bedroom. She didn't sleep, thinking how things went wrong with the Mountain Cow. "These are the hardships that go with farming. People working in jobs don't have upsets like this" she thought.

Then she heard a strange sound coming from the byre.

"It's the moan of a cow in trouble," she said to herself.

"I am not leaving bed again" she thought, "no matter what happens".

Then there was another moan and another. Sarah was now in a state of fear. She got out of bed and put on her warm coat. She kept this close at hand for when she had to leave bed quickly. She came down the stairs again and into the kitchen. Now she must go to the byre.

Stricken with fear, she got the flash lamp, went out into the cold frosty air of the December night and made the short distance to the byre. At first, she was afraid to open the door.

Then she thought to herself, "I must do it as there is no one else here".

She picked up all the courage she had, opened the byre door and shone the flash lamp. There was the Mountain Cow lying on her back in the groop. She had been struggling to get on her feet, rolled off the stand and into the groop. Sarah knew she would not last long in this position. The moans were getting weaker and the breathing heavier. Sarah was desperate as to what to do.

"I must call Whiz even though he is hardly in bed yet".

She made the short distance back to the house and to the phone in the hall. She was hardly able to dial the numbers of the phone, she was so confused. She managed to get through to McNally's, Whiz's father – in – law's house. Whiz was making a bottle for his young son, otherwise he would have been in bed. He answered the phone.

"It's Mother", she said, "Whiz, the Mountain Cow has tumbled off the stand and is on her back in the groop."

Whiz knew this was serious and that the cow would die within a short time in this position. He knew he would not be able to get her turned over without help. As quick as he could, he ran the stairs in McNally's and roused his two young brothers – in – law who were fast asleep. He told them he needed their help back up at Sarah's house. They got out of bed and in a minute were in Whiz's car. Whiz drove fast. They didn't exchange any words as they were still half asleep. Sarah was now standing at the byre door waiting for Whiz.

Every minute seemed like an hour. She could hear the heavy breathing of the cow but the moans had ceased. Then she saw the lights of Whiz's car shining through the tall tree tops that paved the way leading to Sarah's house. She knew that this was Whiz as it was unlikely that any other car would be coming the avenue at three o' clock in the morning. He drove in on the street in a flash.

Whiz asked Sarah "is she still alive?"

"She is but be quick"

All three rushed into the byre and with all the strength in their bodies they rolled the Mountain Cow back on her belly. The heavy breathing ceased and relief came all round. Whiz and Sarah wondered what they were going to do as they knew the same thing would happen again. Whiz told his two brothers – in – law that they could go home and he would stay with Sarah until day break. Then they would decide what they would do with the Mountain Cow.

Sarah whispered to Whiz, "the dead calf has to be buried". This was a hard job to do.

Whiz said to Sarah "we'll go down to the bottom of the

garden where the dale trees are and see if we can find a suitable spot".

They went down and found a spot. "You stay there and I will go up and get the pick and shovel".

In a couple of minutes Whiz was back with the tools.

He started to dig, Sarah holding the flash lamp as it was still dark. He dug for nearly an hour as a lot of big stones came in his way.

Sarah thought to herself "if anyone going past sees us, they'll say there is a ghost in Sarah's garden under the dale trees."

"That hole is deep enough" said Sarah to Whiz.

"I am better make it deep" said Whiz. "I don't want dogs tearing him up after a while, anyhow, he is a big calf".

Whiz made sure he had the hole big enough before he stopped digging. They wondered how they were going to get the dead calf down to the bottom of the garden.

"I will be able to drag him" said Whiz.
"I think you should get the tractor" said Sarah.

"It's all down – hill" said Whiz. "I'll manage without the tractor. The tractor has not been started for two months now and it will be hard to start."

Whiz got a rope, tied it on the dead calf's legs and started to drag the calf to the bottom of the garden. Sarah was too tired to help him. It was more difficult to drag the calf than Whiz thought. He had to rest many times. Sarah showed him the light with the flash lamp. Whiz had the calf at the brow of the hole. He took the rope off the calf's legs and rolled him into the deep hole. They both lamented the loss of the calf. Whiz took the shovel and started to fill back the mould and big stones.

It was back to the byre now to have a look at the Mountain Cow. She was comfortable and chewing the cud. Sarah wondered what they were going to do. They couldn't stand and watch her all the time. That was impossible. Then there were the other cows to be milked.

"How about putting her out in the dry field" said Whiz. "There would be no danger of her getting on her back there and we will have to get some sleep tonight.

"That's what we'll do" said Sarah. "We will have to wait until day light and we will have to get some help".

2
The Dry Field

Because of the difficult calving, the Mountain Cow was paralysed. Sarah and Whiz knew it would be a long time before she stood up and walked, if ever. They both left the byre and stood on the street. Sarah knew that day light was near. She could hear the pheasant calling in the distance and the squirrel was jumping in the branches. She could see smoke rising from the chimney of the house beyond the dry field.

"We will wait another hour before calling Christy" said Sarah.

"We will need Tom as well", said Whiz. "She is a heavy cow and will give us no help".

Sarah went into the house. She riddled up the stove and put on turf and sticks. She put the pan on the stove and when it was hot, put on bacon, sausages and then eggs. She had some soda bread to go with it. She went to the door and called Whiz into breakfast.

"I will call Christy and Tom", said Whiz. Breakfast was over now and Sarah was busy washing up the delph. Whiz took a rest on the couch for a short while.

They went out on the street and the bell was ringing out at the chapel across the hills. Sarah and Whiz blessed themselves and silently said the Angelus. Whiz walked across the dry field to get Christy and Tom. When Christy saw Whiz coming, he wondered what was wrong.

Whiz told Christy he was thinking of "putting the Mountain Cow out on the to the dry field, as she had got on her back in the groop and almost died".

Christy agreed she would be safer there and said, "I will go down shortly".

Whiz then went and asked Tom and told him his intentions. Tom said he would be over as soon as he finished taking tea. Whiz came back to the house to get the tractor ready. Whiz wondered how he was going to get the tractor started. It wasn't started in two months now. He'd put hot water in the radiator and leave it to warm up the engine. He thought of lighting a couple of paper bags and putting them underneath. But that was a dangerous thing to do, he could burn the whole lot. He tried the key in the ignition. But it was dead.

"I'll wait until Christy and Tom come and we will push her".

He saw Christy and Tom coming across the dry field.

"It seems he can't get the tractor started" said Christy.

"We'll have a bit of pushing" said Tom.

They had arrived and Whiz told them he couldn't get the tractor started.

"We'll give her a push" said Christy.

They pushed the tractor out of the shed and over to the top of the hill. Whiz got on the seat, Christy and Tom pushing and when she was near the bottom of the hill, off she went. Whiz revved up the engine. He went back up to the house with the tractor and put on the buck-rake. He then put some boards on the buck-rake and spread some straw over the boards. This was how he was going to take the Mountain Cow to the dry field.

Whiz reversed the tractor over to the byre door. He couldn't get the tractor into the byre as the door was too narrow. Christy and Tom were inside the byre. Whiz tried to get the tractor as close as possible to the byre door. When the tractor was in the right position, Whiz switched off the engine and went into the byre. Sarah stood at the door looking in.

"We will have to take her very easy" said Christy "and I am afraid she isn't going to give us much help".

Christy, Tom and Whiz bent down and clasped their hands underneath the cow.

"Don't lift until I count to three" said Whiz. "One, two, three, heave", but with all the strength they had, they were unable to budge the Mountain Cow. "We will have to get more help," Whiz said to Sarah.

"I will call Paddy and Jim" said Sarah.

Paddy and Jim lived on the other end of the townland across the New Line. The New Line was a new stretch of roadway that the Council made. They came immediately and went into the byre. They talked about the Mountain Cow.

Then Christy said "come on now and we'll try and lift her or we will be here all day".

They bent down and clasped their hands underneath the cow. "One, two, three, heave" and with all their strength they moved her a couple of inches.

"It's great what a bit of power can do" said Christy.

"We have a long way to go still" said Whiz. Inch by inch they moved the Mountain Cow until they had her at the buck-rake.

"Get her knees up first on the boards and then we will swing her round" said Christy.

At last the Mountain Cow was firmly on the buck-rake. Whiz got on the tractor.

"Now drive at a snail's pace" instructed Christy.

Tom stayed on the buck-rake to keep an eye on her. Slowly they all set out for the dry field four hundred yards away. Sarah stayed behind.

It was now Christmas Eve and Sarah had no preparations made for Christmas. Soon her daughters Dot and Dile would arrive. They too had jobs and lived in the city. Just then Dot drove on to the street. She knew when she looked at Sarah that something was wrong.

"What is it?" she said to Sarah.

"It's the Mountain Cow" said Sarah. "She had a difficult calving. The calf is dead and the cow is paralysed."

Dot wished Sarah would stop what she was at, there was too much hardship in it at her age. She went into the house. She knew she would have to prepare for Christmas. Soon afterwards Dile arrived. Dot told her what had happened.

They both set about preparing for Christmas. Sarah wrote out a list of everything they needed for Christmas and Dot went into the town. Dile was busy cleaning the windows and dusting. She looked forward to a rest at Christmas, instead it was plenty of hard work.

In the meantime, Whiz was back. He had left the Mountain Cow under the sheltered hedge in the dry field. All the men were gone home.

"Go straight to bed" he told Sarah. "You need some rest. I'll give another look at the Mountain Cow and I'll take an early night myself".

Sarah told him she would soon go to bed. She knew Whiz would go to stay at his father – in – law's house as his wife and young son were there.

Meanwhile Dot and Dile had the house prepared for Christmas. They even had a Christmas tree in the window. Sarah praised them for having the house so nice. She said good night and slowly climbed the long winding stairs to her bedroom in the far end of the house. She hoped she would sleep tonight. She thought about the Mountain Cow and how things went wrong. She wondered how she would spend the night under the sheltered hedge in the dry field. She wouldn't get on her back there.

Sarah slept well and was up early. It was Christmas morning. Dot, Dile and Sarah went to Mass in the small nearby chapel. A few friends asked Sarah how the Mountain Cow was. Sarah told them she was in the dry field under the sheltered hedge. It was home from Mass now. Dot and Dile made breakfast.

This was the time Sarah enjoyed most. Whiz would be in any minute and they all rested and chatted a while. Dile played a couple of Sarah's favourite records.

Breakfast was over now and Whiz suggested that Sarah and himself would go to look after the Mountain Cow.

"I'd better get the tractor and bring her a few days of fodder" said Whiz "and she would need some meal as well".

Sarah would have to milk her. Whiz never milked a cow by hand. She would have to take a bucket. They both set off on the tractor round the lane by the mill that led to the dry field. They went in the gate and up along the sheltered hedge to where the Mountain Cow was lying. There was no change. Her eyes were bright and she cocked her ears when she saw them coming. Whiz opened one bag of fodder and gave her half of it. She started eating it in great mouthfuls.

"I'll give her the meal now" said Sarah "and I am better start milking her".

Sarah had milked cows by hand when she was young but hadn't milked any for years. She started to milk. It was difficult getting around all four teats when the cow was lying. The milk was flowing from her.

"She was always a great milker," Sarah thought to herself. She managed to get around all four teats. The bucket was full and Sarah wondered what she would do with the milk. "Give it back to the cow to drink" said Whiz.

Sarah thought that was a good idea. It would help to make her strong and put some calcium in her bones. At first, the cow hesitated, but after licking her lips she drank the full bucket of milk without stopping.

"It is better to get her some water as well" said Sarah. Whiz went down to the river, took a bucket of water from it and gave it to the Mountain Cow. She drank it and he went down for another. This time she drank half of it. Sarah and Whiz stood and watched her and wondered when would she rise.

"We will go" said Whiz "for we can do no more for her". They went back on the tractor to the house.

It was a lovely Christmas day. The sun had come out.

Everywhere was peaceful and quiet except for the rush of the water in the river. Back at the house Dot and Dile were busy getting the Christmas dinner ready. They had a turkey cooking in the oven of the stove and ham boiling on the top. They had Brussel sprouts, carrots and peas already cooked.

"We will have dinner at four o'clock," said Dot and she told Whiz to put turf and sticks in the stove as she wanted a good fire until all was cooked. Dile put a white table-cloth on the table. The white table-cloth was used for special occasions and set the table.

Whiz went to McNally's to take his wife Mary and young son to Sarah for Christmas dinner. It was four o'clock now and dinner was ready, the table looked beautiful. There were two candles lit and a bowl of flowers in the centre. Whiz, Mary and the little boy were there.

They all blessed themselves and sat down to dinner. It tasted magnificent and they celebrated with a drink of wine that Dile had brought.

"If Cormac was here now," said Sarah, "we would all be together."

Cormac, Sarah's youngest son, emigrated to America two years ago.

"He will be coming home in the New Year," she told herself.

They all enjoyed dinner but Sarah couldn't help thinking of the Mountain Cow.
As evening approached Sarah said to Whiz, "we are better go back to see the Mountain Cow before night fall." They both set out again.

This time they walked across the dry field. The dry field was a big field, ten acres in all. It always kept dry no matter how much rain came. Cattle always had a dry place to lie down. The Mountain Cow was at the far end of it where the sheltered hedge was. When she saw Sarah and Whiz coming, she cocked her ears. Now they were with her again. Whiz gave her a bag of fodder and Sarah bent down and milked her. They gave the milk to her to drink. Whiz gave her a bucket of water from the river but she didn't drink it.

"We will go back now before it gets dark," said Sarah. Slowly they walked back up the dry field, the years starting to show on Sarah. As they walked, they wondered if they should get Mr. Geff to have another look at her.

"I'll call him tomorrow," said Whiz.

It was now the second day of Christmas. Sarah and Whiz did the same thing – went to the Mountain Cow, gave her fodder, milked her and gave her the milk to drink. Whiz took the bucket of water from the river and gave it to her. "Did you call Mr. Geff?" asked Sarah.

"He will be here sometime today," said Whiz.

"I wonder will he be able to do anything for her?", said Sarah.

Sarah and Whiz made their way across the dry field to the house. In a short time Mr. Geff arrived at Sarah's house in the Land Rover. He went straight into the byre but the Mountain Cow wasn't there. Whiz went out quickly and told him he had moved her out to the dry field along the sheltered hedge. Whiz explained to Mr. Geff that she was getting on her back in the byre and thought it was safer to put her in the dry field. Mr. Geff agreed she was safer in the dry field.

"She will have more space to manoeuvre there. Hop into the Land Rover," Mr. Geff told Whiz, "and we will drive round by the mill to have a look at her."

Sarah remained at the house. She knew Whiz would tell her what Mr. Geff thought of the Mountain Cow. She waited anxiously for Whiz to return. She put turf and sticks in the stove and made herself a mug of tea. She looked out and saw Whiz coming across the dry field.

"Mr. Geff must be gone," she thought.
Before Whiz quite reached the house, Sarah asked him,
"what did Mr. Geff think of her?".

"He didn't say much," was the reply. "He gave me a bottle
of medicine for her, one half tonight and the other half
tomorrow."

"I hope it does her some good," said Sarah.

Soon Whiz would go back to his job in the city. Dot and
Dile would be leaving too and Sarah would be on her own.
"How was she going to cope looking after the Mountain
Cow? She would have to do her best", Sarah thought to
herself.

Whiz was worried about how Sarah would manage when
he was gone. "I'll leave six or seven bags of fodder over
in the dry field," said Whiz. "It will do her a few days.

Christy will bring some fodder as well".

Sarah would have the task of milking the cow, morning and evening. Cormac would be coming home from New York in the New Year. Sarah told Cormac about the Mountain Cow in a letter. He too worked on the small farm before going to New York. He often brought the cows home to the byre to be milked.

It was now the month of January. Whiz was gone back to his job in the city. Dot and Dile were leaving in the morning. Sarah wished they could stay but she knew that wasn't possible. Sarah would be on her own now.
She would have to go twice daily to look after the Mountain Cow. "Would she walk across the dry field or ride the bike round by the mill?"

She would have to take the bucket to milk the cow and a couple of pounds of meal. She thought to herself that it was best to go on the bike. "I will put the meal in a small bag and put it in the bucket, then put the bucket on the handlebars. I will have to be careful in case of falling off the bike," she thought.

The following morning after everyone was gone, Sarah set out on the bike round by the mill. She put the bucket on the handlebars with the meal in a small bag inside. It was a cold morning with patches of frost. The squirrels were everywhere, running in front of Sarah and then disappearing into the hedge. Sarah thought of the Mountain Cow, unable to rise.

But she consoled herself that at least she had shelter. When she got to the dry field Christy was there. He knew Whiz had left.

He dragged over one of the bags of fodder Whiz had left in the dry field and gave it to her. Sarah gave her the meal and bent down and milked her. Tom arrived.

"I'll get her a bucket of water" said Tom. He went down to the river, took a bucket of water from it, gave it to her and went for another. Sarah gave her the milk to drink. They looked at her for a few minutes. Sarah thanked Christy and Tom and they all left. As Sarah rode the bike back by the mill, she thought of having to go back in the evening to do the same thing again.

3
The Strange Dog

Whiz came home at the weekends and helped Sarah. The month of January was nearly gone and still no sign of the Mountain Cow to rise. Then one day a strange dog came to Sarah's house. He was black with white belly, white paws and a white band round his neck. He was fully grown and about one year old. He had a rope round his neck that was frayed at the ends. Sarah wondered where he came from or who owned him.

He was very thin and it was easy to count his ribs. He didn't come close to Sarah. He always kept about ten yards away. Sarah thought to herself that she couldn't let him stay as it was too dangerous to keep a big dog like that, so she run him off.

The next morning when Sarah got out of bed and looked out of the window the big black dog with white belly, paws and white band round the neck was lying underneath the big beech tree. Sarah dressed herself and went down the long winding stairs into the kitchen. She made herself a quick mug of tea, got on the bike, put the bucket on the handlebars and went around by the mill to look after the Mountain Cow.

When the dog saw Sarah going on the bike, he got up from under the big beech tree and followed her all the way to the dry field. Sarah dragged over a bag of fodder to the Mountain Cow, got her a bucket of water from the river, bent down and milked her and gave her the milk to drink.

The dog was in the dry field, sitting ten yards away. The Mountain Cow always left a small licking of milk in the bottom of the bucket. Sarah thought she would give the dog the bucket to lick. She put the bucket down and walked away about ten yards.

Then the dog came and licked the bucket. Sarah left the dog ten yards behind her. When Sarah reached the house, he went to lie under the beech tree. Tomorrow, Sarah would ask Christy and Tom if anybody lost a dog.

It was now February and Cormac would soon be home from New York. He would help Sarah look after the Mountain Cow. Sarah knew he couldn't milk by hand so she still would have the task of milking her. Some days Sarah rode the bike, other days she walked across the dry field, the strange dog always following her ten yards behind. She asked Christy and Tom if they knew who owned the dog. But they didn't. Sarah always gave him the bucket to lick after the Mountain Cow had finished drinking the milk.

Then one day Cormac arrived. He came in a big car hired

out at the airport. Sarah was so happy to see him and he was glad to be home again with Sarah. He told her about New York and all the Irish that were there.

He helped Sarah morning and evening with the Mountain Cow. He took several bags of fodder on the tractor.

One day Cormac was in the town and he heard a Reilly man had an apparatus for lifting cows. This man lived the other side of the town. It was a huge rubber bag that was put underneath the cow but as there was no electricity in the dry field, they would have to bring the Mountain Cow back again to one of the sheds. She knew she couldn't go into the old byre with the groops. There was the shed that Sarah kept her bike and a small trailer in.

"They could be moved somewhere else and put down a good bed of straw" said Sarah.

Cormac said "I will go and ask Reilly if he would come and lift her".

Cormac set out to find Reilly. He knew he lived about two miles the other side of the town. After inquiring off a few people he found him.

He asked if he would come and lift the Mountain Cow. Reilly said he would come the following day around two o'clock.

Cormac came back without delay as he knew he had to take the Mountain Cow back to the shed. He got the tractor, put on the buck-rake, put some boards on the buck-rake and finally some straw. He called Christy, Tom, Paddy and Jim to help him get her loaded up on the buck-rake. Christy, Tom, Jim and Paddy bent down, clasped their hands underneath the cow and with one mighty heave they landed her on the buck-rake.

Cormac drove back by the mill at snail's pace with Tom on the buck-rake, keeping a watchful eye on her in case she fell off. Sarah was in the house watching out the window to see the return of the Mountain Cow. Slowly the tractor came around the corner and up the hill to the house. Cormac reversed the tractor over to the shed door, let down the buck- rake and gently rolled the Mountain Cow in on the nice bed of straw.

Sarah was happy to have her in the shed. She would be finished riding the bike round by the mill or walking across the dry field with the strange dog ten yards behind. The following day Reilly came with the apparatus for lifting cows. Christy, Tom, Jim and Paddy came as well. The huge rubber bag was worked in underneath the belly of the cow. There was a pump attached to one end of the bag and it was plugged into the electricity. It started to pump air into the bag and as the bag rose higher with the air, the Mountain Cow started to rise up as well. When Reilly had the bag pumped high enough and her legs were just touching the ground, he asked Sarah to bring him a couple of buckets of hot water and four cloths. He soaked the cloths in the water and told Christy, Tom, Paddy and Jim to start massaging her legs with the cloths that were soaked in the hot water.

"This will help to bring back circulation in her legs" said Reilly. He asked Sarah to renew the hot water.

Reilly kept the cow in this position for around fifteen minutes. Then he slowly let the air out of the bag and she was back on the ground again. Reilly was leaving now. He didn't hold out much hope for the Mountain Cow, but told Cormac and Sarah to keep massaging her legs. All the others were leaving too.

Christy suggested to the others that they should all come and lift her for one week "until we see what happens".

They said that "it would be very difficult to do".

"We'll give it a try" said Christy.

They all agreed to come to Sarah's shed to lift the Mountain Cow at two o'clock the following day. The following day was Saturday and Whiz was there to help with the lifting. At two o'clock all the men arrived. Some came in cars and others on tractors. They all went into the shed. They all stood wondering which was the best way to lift her. Then Whiz and Cormac and the others bent down and got their hands underneath the cow.

"One, two, three" said Whiz "heave".

"We have her up" shouted Christy. "See that her legs are propped" he said.

Whiz and Cormac got fresh handfuls of straw and rubbed her legs to help the circulation. She swayed from side to side, but the men kept her steady. Sarah thought it would be a good time to milk her when the men were holding her up, so she got the bucket and milked her. She gave her the milk to drink and then the bucket to the strange dog, who was ten yards away, to lick. They kept her up for fifteen minutes and then gently let her down on a fresh bed of straw. Some of the men didn't hold out much hope for her. "Would she ever stand up on her own and walk again?" We'll lift her for one week" said Christy, "until we see what happens".

"Good enough" said all the others.

For a week they all came and lifted the Mountain Cow.

When the week was up Christy said "the lifting doesn't seem to be doing her any good so we will call it off". Sarah thanked them all for coming and said "you all did your best".

Some of the men thought she would have to be put down. Others wondered "would Sarah get anything for her in the factory?" Whiz knew Sarah didn't like to hear this.

The month of February was gone and it was the beginning of March. Cormac would soon be leaving for New York. The snowdrops were in full bloom. The daffodils were well up. The mill-race flowed all around Sarah's house, the old mill, with the spring well beside it, still standing, the apple garden and the beech trees budding. New York had nothing to compare to this - he would be back in a while.

Cormac went to leave goodbye with Christy and Tom and finally with Sarah. He would leave goodbye with Whiz, Dot and Dile in the city.

Sarah stood by the window and watched him drive away. She turned away from the window and put sticks and turf on the stove. She took the chair with the short legs and sat by the stove and a lot of her life on the small farm flashed back into her head. The strange dog was no longer a stranger. He sneaked up to Sarah, put his head under her arm and laid his head on her lap.

Sarah thought about when Pat and her first married, how they won the hay, set the potatoes and cabbage, milked the cows by hand, went to the fair with the cattle, kept the hens and turkeys, drained the fields.

She thought of the times when the four children were born

in the house, how they walked the two miles to school, always wearing the wellingtons in Winter and of how she washed the yellow clay from the wellingtons to have them ready for the next day. She thought of the times further back when they had no electricity and had the old Morris Minor. That was all history now so Sarah thought she had better get up and look after the Mountain Cow.

4
The Cure

Then one day James arrived. James was an old man who lived across the river. He kept a small boat for crossing the river. He always came once a year to visit Sarah. He heard about the Mountain Cow being unable to rise and came to tell Sarah to get the cure made. Sarah was glad to see James. He stayed all day and had dinner with Sarah. They talked about the ups and downs on the land and about emigration. Sarah said it was sad to see so many young people leaving.

As dusk was falling James said he would go as he would

like to get across the river before dark. He warned Sarah to get the cure made.

He told her that "there was a woman who lived at the bottom of the town who made the cure". He knew a man who had it made for a cow that was lying and she was up the next day.

When Whiz came home at the weekend, Sarah told him that James came on a visit and told her to get the cure made for the Mountain Cow. Sarah asked Whiz if he would go to the woman and ask her to make the cure. "Who makes it?" enquired Whiz.

"It's Molly, she lives at the bottom of the town" said Sarah. Whiz said he would go and ask her in the morning. The next morning Whiz went into the town and asked Molly if she would come and make the cure for the Mountain Cow. Molly told him she had certain days for making the cure and that she would come on Tuesday evening.

Whiz thanked her and told her how she would get to Sarah's. On Tuesday evening Molly arrived at Sarah's. Sarah took her to the shed where the Mountain Cow was lying.

"How long is she lying?" Molly inquired from Sarah.

"Three months" Sarah told her.

Then she bent down, blessed the Mountain Cow, laid her hands on her and prayed. Sarah remained silent. When Molly had finished making the cure, she told Sarah to give her more time and to keep the legs massaged.

It was the month of April and Sarah was getting very worried about what she was going to do with the Mountain Cow.

"If only she would stand up" she thought.

The weather was getting warmer and there was a nice bud

of grass coming on the fields. Sarah thought if she had the Mountain Cow taken out again to the field, the Spring grass would help her.

She talked with Whiz and they decided to take her to the small field at the back of the byre. This field was close to the house and it would be handy for Sarah looking after her.

"We will give her one last chance" said Whiz.

He called Christy and Tom and told them. They didn't think it would be any use, but they would help him get her to the small field. The following morning Christy and Tom arrived. Whiz got the tractor ready and put the buck-rake on, put boards and straw on the buck-rake. He reversed the tractor to the shed door. By this time the Mountain Cow was getting use to being lifted.

When they had her on the buck-rake, Whiz drove the tractor to the small field at the back of the byre. Christy and Tom kept a watchful eye on her on the buck-rake. When they reached the field, Whiz lowered the buck-rake and gently laid her down on a nice dry bank. The sun was shining and she started eating the grass that was around her.

"That will do her good" said Christy.

A week passed and Whiz was home at the weekend. He took a few bags of fodder and left them in the field. He gave one bag to the Mountain Cow. Sarah went with the bucket and the small bag with the nuts. The strange dog was walking close to Sarah. She milked the Mountain Cow, gave her the milk to drink and then the bucket to the strange dog to lick.

When the weekend passed Whiz went back to the city and Sarah, now with her close companion, the strange dog, were as usual going to look after the Mountain Cow. Suddenly one day as Sarah walked up to her, she cocked her ears, let out a "loo" and got on her knees. Sarah never saw her do this before. The following day when she saw Sarah coming, she got on her knees and made a great plunge to get on her feet, but slumped back on the ground. Sarah thought to herself, "she is surely making progress".

When Whiz came at the weekend Sarah told him what she saw the Mountain Cow doing. Whiz said he would go to see her. Sarah went with him and as they were walking up to her, she made a great plunge and got on her feet. Whiz ran to her and helped to steady her with his hands. Sarah couldn't believe what she was seeing.

"It's a miracle, it's a miracle" she shouted.

Whiz kept her steady with his hands. She stayed up for twenty minutes and then lay down. The next day when she saw Sarah coming, she did the same thing, made a great plunge and got on her feet. This time she started eating grass.

"It's unbelievable" Sarah thought to herself as she stood and watched her.

Then Sarah went to tell Christy and Tom.

"The Mountain Cow is on her feet" she told them, but they wouldn't believe her.

"Come and see for yourselves" said Sarah.

Christy and Tom came and when they saw her on her feet, they were speechless.

"How long was she lying for?" asked Christy.

"Four months" said Sarah.

They had no words to say.

The Mountain Cow stayed in the field at the back of the byre for some time. By this time, she was walking about through the field and eating the nice fresh Spring grass. Sarah wrote to Cormac in New York and told him the good news about the Mountain Cow.

Then one day Sarah and Whiz decided to take her back to the byre where her comrades were. This time there would be no need for the tractor. They opened the gate and drove her out on to the old crab lane and as she walked along, she stopped to have a drink in the stream and then on again. Sarah and Whiz walked proudly behind her to the byre door. She hesitated for a minute before going in and up to her place by the wall. Sarah put the chain around her neck.

The Mountain Cow took a long look at Sarah and Whiz. She was happy to be back in her old spot by the wall. Sarah and Whiz were happy too.

"Let's all celebrate the rise of the Mountain Cow" said Sarah.